Horse Rescue!

by Jiang Qingling
illustrated by Carlotta Tormey

PEARSON

Scott
Foresman

Editorial Offices: Glenview, Illinois • Parsippany, New Jersey • New York, New York
Sales Offices: Needham, Massachusetts • Duluth, Georgia • Glenview, Illinois
Coppell, Texas • Ontario, California • Mesa, Arizona

March 7, 2001
Coast Guard Rescues Horses

A bad storm can hit with rolling thunder and lightning flashes. Sometimes animals are in danger because of such a storm. The Coast Guard is a group that rescues people or animals that are in danger in the water.

On March 7, 2001, the Coast Guard rescued twelve horses from a flood on a farm in Monroe, Louisiana. The farm was normally a sunny place with pretty hills, but this day was dark and stormy. Rain pounded down.

It rained for so long that the rivers filled up. Water poured onto the land. The land began to flood.

The farmers tried to take the horses to a safe place, but twelve horses were trapped in deep water.

The farmers called the United States Coast Guard for help. The Coast Guard had to make a plan to save the horses. They usually did not rescue such large animals.

The Coast Guard used boats and helicopters. They also used slings that were made just for horses. They also called animal doctors to take care of the horses.

Helicopters flew to the place where the horses were last seen. By this time the water came up to the horses' backs and even their necks!

The Coast Guard flew into the storm to get to the horses. They loaded the smaller horses onto a boat. They moved the boat to dry land, where the horses would be safe.

The Coast Guard used helicopters to save the big horses. First, they flew above the horses. Rain poured down, but they kept going. Next, they sent a person down to help each horse into a sling.

When the horse was in the sling, the helicopter lifted it high into the air! The helicopters carried each horse to dry land. Veterinarians made sure the horses were not hurt.

Storms and floods can be very dangerous. The horses in Monroe were lucky the Coast Guard was there to help. Thanks to a good plan and hard work, the horses were safe and dry at last!